# The Joy of Waltzes, Tan and Polkas

### Selected and arranged by Denes Agay.

Cover design by Mike Bell Design, London

This book Copyright © 1998 by Yorktown Music Press, Inc.

Order No. YK 21842
US International Standard Book Number: 978.0.8256.8103.5
UK International Standard Book Number: 0.7119.6775.X

Yorktown Music Press, Inc.

# Contents

# Viennese Waltz

Ludwig van Beethoven

# Schubert Gallery

Franz Schubert

# Invitation to the Dance

Carl Maria von Weber

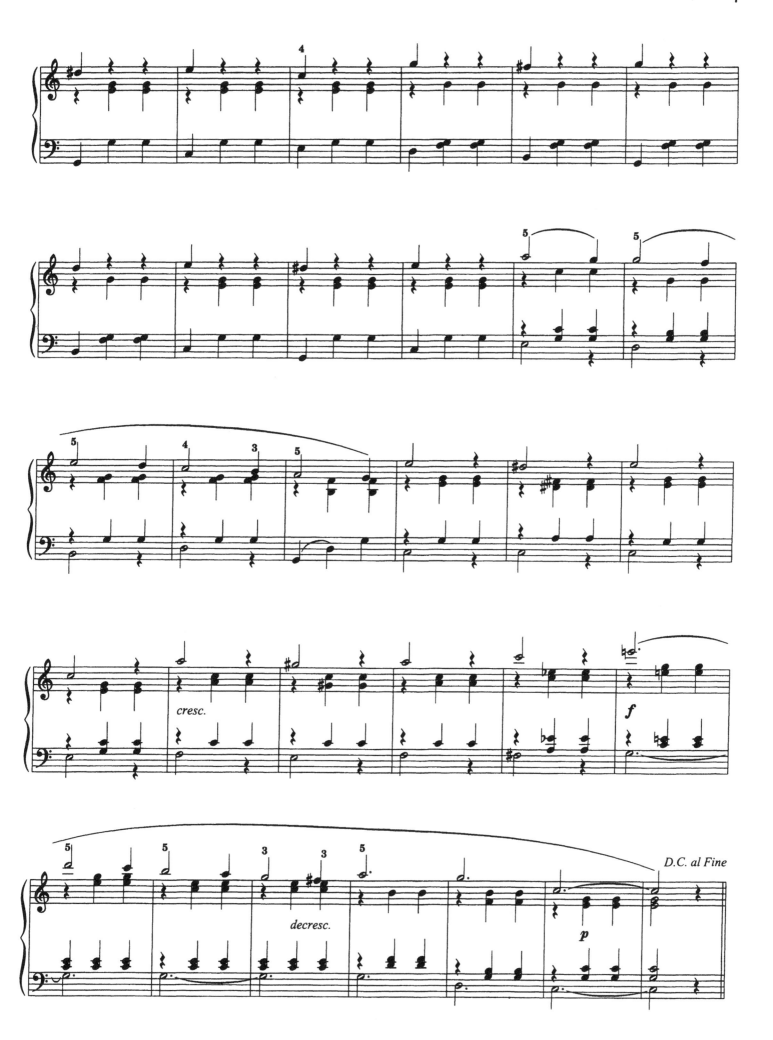

# Chopin Mosaics

(Waltz Themes)

Frederic Chopin

# Waltz

Johannes Brahms

# Waltzes by Strauss

"The Emperor Waltz"

Johann Strauss

"Vienna Life"

"Wine, Women, and Song"

# Valse Lente

from *"Coppelia"*

Leo Delibes

# Waltz of the Flowers
## from *"The Nutcracker"*

Peter I. Tchaikovsky

# The "Sleeping Beauty" Waltz

(Theme)

Peter I. Tchaikovsky

# Waltz from "Faust"

Charles Gounod

# Waltz from "Fledermaus"

Johann Strauss

# Love's Sorrow

*Liebesleid*

Fritz Kreisler

# Melodic Gems in ¾ Time

### Waltz Themes from the Golden Age of Operetta

"Opera Ball"

Richard Heuberger

"Countess Dubarry"

Edited by Denes Agay

Karl Millöcker

## "Eva"

Franz Lehàr

## "Sari"

Emmerich Kálmán

# The "Merry Widow" Waltz

Franz Lehár

# Waltz from "Der Rosenkavalier"

Richard Strauss

# Estudiantina

Emile Waldteufel

# Hesitation Waltz

from *"The Red Poppy"*

Reinhold Glière

# Sympathy Waltz

from *"The Firefly"*

Rudolf Friml

# Will You Remember

from *"Sweetheart"*

Sigmund Romberg

# Ragtime Waltz

*"Pleasant Moments"*

Scott Joplin

# Tango

Isaac Albeniz

# Tango Argentina

*A Media Luz*

E. Donato

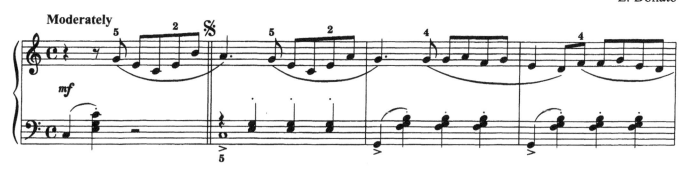

# Brazilian Tango

*Brejeiro*

Ernesto Nazareth

**Allegretto**

# Forbidden Dreams

(Tango Continental)

Denes Agay

2nd time To Coda ⊕

# El Choclo

A. G. Villoldo

# La Cumparsita

C. H. Matos Rodriguez

**Marked, moderate tempo**

# Tango d'Amour

Gerald Martin

# La Rosita

Paul Dupont

CHORUS

# Jalousie

(Tango Tzigane)

Jacob Gade

# Adios Muchachos

Julio Sanders

# Tango Intermezzo

Denes Agay

**Moderato; with a steady beat**

# Russian Polka

Michael Ivanovich Glinka

# Swedish Polka

Theme from *"Swedish Rhapsody"*

Hugo Alfvén

# Krakowiak

(Polish Polka)

Traditional

# The "Merry Boys" Polka

Franz von Suppé

# The "Fledermaus" Polka

Johann Strauss

# Clarinet Polka

Traditional
Rev. by Denes Agay

# Pizzicato Polka

from *"Sylvia"*

Leo Delibes

# Polka from "The Bartered Bride"

Bedrich Smetana

# Polka Italiana

Arranged by Gerald Martin

E. di Capua
L. Denza

# Gypsy Polka

Denes Agay

# Helena Polka

Continental Melody

# The Fanny Schneider Polka

Traditional
Rev. by Gerald Martin

# Hurry Up, Harry

Jimmy Eaton
Denes Agay

2. You left a ladder beside the garden gate,
Oh, how romantic, oh, Harry don't be late,
Me and my trousseau, bows and buttons too,
Are right by the window, waiting for you!

*Chorus*

3. The same ladder lingers beside the garden wall
Covered with ivy but nothin's changed at all
Only my trousseau will soon be out of date,
Tell me how much longer will I have to wait?

*Chorus*

# There Is A Tavern In The Town

Traditional

**Lively Polka**

1. There is a tav-ern in the town, in the town, And there my dear love sits him down, sits him down, __ And __ drinks his wine 'mid laugh-ter __ free, And nev-er nev-er thinks of me. __ Fare thee

Chorus

well, for I must leave thee, Do not let the part - ing grieve thee, And re -

mem - ber that the best of friends must part, must part. A - dieu, a -

dieu, kind friends, a - dieu, a - dieu, a - dieu; I can no long - er stay with

you, stay with you; I'll hang my harp on a weep - ing wil - low

tree, And may the world go well with thee.